Never Make an Uninformed Financial Decision Again

Book 3: An Adult Relationship with Money

by Hayden Burrus

Table of Contents

Chapter 1 - Borrowing - Is it a Good Idea?

Borrowing is a good idea <u>if</u> your cash flow improves after you take out the loan. That's pretty rare. Borrowing to buy a car is out. Owning a car doesn't improve cash flow. Borrowing for furniture or a vacation are also out. Borrowing to pay for an education or a house are definite maybes. Just a maybe? Yup!

Borrowing to buy something results in your paying more than everyone else for that purchase because borrowers must pay interest in exchange for having it now. It's poor money management to pay more than you have to for something. That's why borrowing is generally a bad idea. Borrowers seem to never be able to get ahead because they end up paying more for everything they buy. Borrowers pay full price and interest too.

Borrowing can be a good idea, however. It is a great idea when it enables you to earn more and / or spend less. Let's take student loans as an example. If a student borrows $10K each year for their college experience, the student will be $46,386 in debt on graduation day. Then, over the next 10 years the college graduate will pay $474/month for a total payment of $56,923 for $40,000 of college. The student is agreeing to pay an extra $16,923 in exchange for getting his education right away. That can be a good idea if the young graduate's earnings can more than make up that shortfall. So, in examining whether it is worthwhile for a young adult with no money to borrow his tuition that young adult must ask himself whether his degree will produce an income improvement larger than the student loan payment. A $474 monthly loan payment comes out to $5,600 per year after taxes or about $7,300 before taxes. Now the consideration of student loans comes down to a simple question-- is the expected income of the college graduate more than $7,300 higher than his expected income if he does not go to college. For many potential career paths, the answer is "Yes". For those, you have my permission to borrow. For some career paths, the answer is "No." In those cases, I recommend you postpone your college plans until you've saved enough money to pay in cash.

How about borrowing to buy a house? Well, borrowing to buy a house is a special case that gets its own chapter in this book. It comes down to cash flows. Borrowing to buy a house is a good idea when your positive cash flows-- saved rent, tax savings-- beats your negative cash flows -- mortgage, property tax, property insurance, repairs, loss of flexibility to move, and major consequences to missing payments.

Borrowing creates leverage. Leverage occurs when you control more assets than you own. Leverage can be great when you are generating a positive return because a positive rate of return on more assets generates more income. For example, If you have $20K and make an investment that generates a 5% return, you are getting $1000 a year in investment income. Not too bad. However, if you have $20K and then borrowed $180K to buy a $200K investment property and then that property generates a 5% return (after interest payments), you are getting $10K in investment income. This is a much better result. When businesses borrow, they are seeking to achieve a result like this. Leverage done poorly can really be financially devastating. If you choose to sell that house in a few years and real estate values are depressed in your area, you might get only $180K. That will pay off your mortgage and there will be nothing left for you. Your $20K investment will have completely disappeared - a minus 100% return on your investment.

Consumer purchases always generate a negative return and borrowing and using leverage to pay for a consumer purchase just amplifies that negative return.

Let's say your net worth is $0. You don't have much in the bank and whatever assets you have are completely offset by credit card debt. Now let's say you buy a $20K car. Hooray, you now have a $20K asset. Your car loan also constitutes a $20K debt so your net worth is still zero. You drive home a happier person. Tomorrow when you wake up you decide to calculate your net worth again. You still owe $20K on your car loan, you look out to the street and estimate that you could sell your car for about $16K. So your net worth has dropped from $0 to minus $4K in just one day. Your car purchase is turning out to be a wealth destroyer.

Chapter 2 - The Income Part of Income Tax

This isn't a chapter on how to do your taxes or how to fill out tax forms. Unless that's your job, that's not your job to know that. There's software you can use, or there's people you can pay to fill out your tax forms. You do need to know about taxes, though. You need to know in general how taxes are calculated so that you can do more things that reduce your taxes and fewer things that increase your taxes.

Income is calculated based on all of your sources of income. The more income you have, the larger the percentage of your income will be paid in taxes. For example, if you have no income at all and you get a $20K increase in income, you will not have to pay any tax at all. You'll keep the whole $20K. The government figures that you need that money. However, if your income is more than $500,000 and you get a $20K increase in income, you'll have to pay $7,920 in income tax back to the government. You'll keep only $12,080 of that money. Here, the government feels you can afford to give a substantial chunk of that raise because you already earned $500K which is more than enough to live on. That's called a progressive income tax rate. The USA has always had a progressive income tax system, however the progressiveness of our tax system has gone up and down over time depending on the mood of our legislators in Washington.

Because the income tax rate is progressive, your tax decisions should be based on the tax rate that your next dollar of income is subject to. This rate is called the "marginal tax rate". More informally many people call it their "tax bracket". The marginal tax rates for people with full time jobs generally range from 15% to 28%. If you are fortunate enough to be in the top 3% or so of family income, taxes will rise to 33% and possibly as high as 39.6%.

Tip #1: Because a smaller percentage of your income is taxed in years where you earn less money, it is worthwhile for you to increase your income in these years if it allows you to decrease your income in a future year.

For example, if you are having a good year this year and are scheduled to be paid in December, you might tell your client to hold off payment until January. If your next year's income is lower, the taxes you pay on that client's invoice payment might be lower. Less taxes paid means more money for you... just for waiting an extra month to get paid.

For most people, their job provides the bulk of their income. Other common sources of income include retirement income, investment income, capital gains, and rental income. Gifts aren't income, and neither are expense reimbursements. Also, when you sell something at breakeven or a loss, there's no income. As a matter of fact, there might even be a deduction. But I am getting ahead of myself.

Each type of income is taxed in a different way, so it's important to understand the differences and increase your focus on income that is taxed the least.

The highest taxed type of income is self employment income (including income statements that are reported on "1099 forms"). That's because this is the only type of income that is taxed three times instead of just once like most other types of income. Of course you pay income tax on your self employment income. As a matter of fact, when calculating your income tax, your self employment income is added to several different types of income to determine income tax. The IRS doesn't distinguish between income types here. However, in addition to the ordinary income tax you pay on this income, there is a special line to calculate the additional "self-employment tax" on your self-employment income. That tax is 12.3% of self employment income. So a self employed person earning $50K per year will pay an additional $6,150 in tax above what he would pay if he earned that money some other way. The thought process behind the self -employment tax is that self-employed people do not pay into social security, so this additional tax makes up for it.

Job income is taxed only slightly less severely. Job income is included with the other types of income to determine your total income tax. In addition to the ordinary income tax arising from your job, you are also required to pay into Social Security and Medicare funds. Presumably you'll get some of this money back when you retire. The total social security and Medicare contribution is 7.65%. That's a little better than the 12.3% additional tax you'd have to pay on your 1099 income, but not much. As an aside, the company you work for is also required to pay 7.65% of your income into Social Security and Medicare on your behalf, but that's not your concern. Your job income is reported to you at the end of the year on a W-2 form.

Tip #2: If you can choose between getting "1099 income" and a paycheck, choose the paycheck. Not only are you more likely to get benefits available only to employees, but you are also able to avoid the self employment tax.

The next category is interest income. It includes savings account, CD, bond, and loan interest you received. This is the most straightforward- It is added on to your other sources of income to determine income tax. There are no additional taxes resulting from that income.

Next are investment gains. When you buy something, anything, and then sell it for more than you bought it for, you experience an investment gain and that is another type of income. Dividends paid for stocks you own are also investment gains. The most common sources of investment gain are from buying and selling stocks or property (including your own home). There are two types of investment gains and they are taxed differently. There are "short-term" investment gains. These gains are from stock dividends or things you sold less than a year after you bought them. They are taxed just like interest income. There are also "long-term" capital gains. Long term investment gains are taxed at a much lower rate than other types of income. As a matter of fact, a married person making less than $90K or so (including investment gains) will not have to pay any tax at all on this income. The most a person would have to pay on long term capital gains tax is 23.8%. That would only occur if the total family income is over $460K or so. A person earning that much will have to pay about 41% on earned income or short term capital gains. So, at any income level, long term capital gains are taxed very favorably.

Tip #3: Whenever possible delay sales of profitable items until after you've owned the item for more than a year so you can take advantage of the long term capital gains tax rate.

Investment gains and losses are allowed to offset each other. So, If you have one investment that gained $20K and another that lost $15K, you would only have to report $5K in investment gains.

Tip #4: In years when you have investment gains, pick an investment that is losing money and sell it. This will reduce your taxes.

Investment gains are only taxed when they are "realized" meaning that you sold the investment and received the money. A buy and hold investor will never pay capital gains tax because they never sell their investments. A person who sells her investment portfolio every year will be paying capital gains tax every year. This practice lowers investment gains and increases your total tax bill over your lifetime.

Tip #4a: Sell your investments infrequently and only if you think your investment will decrease in value.

There is a special rule on investment gains for when you sell your home. The first $500K in investment gains on home sales don't count. For most people that means that they don't have to pay any tax on profits from home sales.

Tip #5: If the value of your home is approaching $500K more than what you paid, you may wish to sell your home and buy a new one to avoid capital gains tax. You can do this over and over again if you are fortunate enough to have homes that appreciate in value by $500K.

Now on to retirement income. Pensions and IRAs are taxed just like investment income (assuming you are older than 59 1/2). If you are under 59 1/2 and are drawing from your IRA, you are taxed worst of all. First, you paid social security tax when you earned the money; second you are paying income tax as described above, and third, you are paying an extra 10% tax as an early withdrawal penalty. If you are single and making more than $44K or so, you'll pay an amazing 42.65% tax on money deposited to an IRA and then withdrawn before you are 59 1/2 (25%

marginal income tax + 7.65% social security + 10% early withdrawal penalty). In addition, your employer paid another 7.65% of that income to social security. Almost 50% of the money you earned is returned back to the IRS.

Tip #6: Don't do that.

The taxes on investment gains and interest income inside of IRAs are zero. That's true no matter how much you earn.

Tip #7: Whenever possible purchase investments that are more likely to generate investment income inside of your IRA instead of with taxable money. That way you don't have to pay tax on the gains.

Roth IRAs are taxed at zero provided that you are over 59 1/2.

Tip 8: If you are of retirement age and you need extra money, withdraw from your Roth IRA first.

Gifts and inheritances are not taxed. If you are fortunate enough to receive either, congratulations!

Only a portion of your Social Security income is taxed, depending on what your income is from other sources. If you have no other sources of income, your Social Security might not be taxed at all. If you have other income sources, as much as 85% of your social security benefit will be included in income for your income tax calculation. Since not all of your social security benefit payments are included in your income, it is taxed more favorably than other types of income. You can decide to begin collecting social security at any time between age 62 and 70. Your benefit check will be a lot higher (almost double) if you wait until age 70.

Tip 9: If you have other sources of savings, wait as long as possible before collecting Social Security. Your income will go up and your tax payments will be delayed.

So this chapter talks about the different ways income is taxed and provides some tips on how to reduce the taxes you pay on your income without reducing your income. Please keep in mind that in no case should you turn down income in order to avoid paying income tax. Income taxes always increase more slowly than income.

Tip 10: Increasing your income always improves your family's bottom line.

The next chapter deals with deductions, which are expenses that you can subtract from your income before calculating income tax.

Chapter 3 - The Deductions Part of Income Tax

The last chapter gave you the knowledge to calculate total income and tips on minimizing what the IRS thinks your total income is. While different types of income are taxed in different ways, they are all added together to get total income. This is the biggest income item on your tax return. Fortunately you don't pay taxes on that number. You pay taxes on your net income which is your total income minus listed deductions minus itemized deductions. It's not uncommon for net income to be $20K or more less than total income.

Listed deductions are better than itemized deductions but not as good as tax credits. Listed deductions are twelve specific types of expenses that you can deduct from your total income no matter what. Itemized deductions are only deductible if you have a lot of them. Credits are the best of all- they are deductions to the tax you pay. A $1000 credit means you pay $1000 less in taxes, while a $1000 deduction reduces your taxable income by a $1000. Your taxes might only be reduced by $150.

The most commonly listed deductions are:

- Teacher supplies (up to $250)
- Health Savings Account or Retirement Plan Contribution (e.g. IRA, 401(k)) (Roth IRA contributions are NOT deductible)

- Moving expenses (for a job)
- Health insurance that you paid for
- Alimony paid (hooray, a deduction for you and income for your ex-spouse)
- Student loan interest (up to $2500)
- College tuition and books (up to $4000)

If you incur any of these expenses it is important to document these expenses and save your receipts so you can properly calculate the deduction at year end. Also you might want to read more details about the expense deductions you think you might qualify for.

Now you have enough knowledge to know how much some of your expenses are really costing you. Take your marginal tax rate (see prior chapter) and multiply it by a listed deduction you are entitled to. This number is how much your taxes are reduced. For example, let's say you paid $10,000 towards college tuition (if you borrow to pay it, it still counts). Your listed deduction is $4000 (that's the max). Now let's say you are in the 25% marginal tax rate. Your taxes are reduced by $1000 ($4000 x 25%). The net cost of the tuition for you is $9000 ($10,000 tuition - $1000 tax savings).

Your total income minus your listed deductions equal your adjusted gross income (AGI). Some tax deductions are phased out depending on your AGI. Don't worry about that for now.

Deductions

The next section is for deductions. Here you have a choice-- you can list itemized deductions, or you can take a "standard deduction"

The standard deduction is $6300 for a single person and $12600 for a married couple. Anyone can choose to deduct this amount from your AGI (which is less than your total income). Your AGI minus your deductions is your taxable income. Below are the most popular items that you can itemize.

- Medical and dental expenses (unreimbursed by insurance and over 10% of your income)
- Property tax
- State income tax
- Sales tax on vehicles, boats, planes, and pre-fab homes (but only if it is more than your state income tax)
- Home mortgage Interest and "points"
- Charitable gifts

Tip 1: If you own your own home, you should definitely be tracking your itemized deductions. If not, you probably shouldn't waste your time.

If you don't have a mortgage on your home, you are probably not going to have enough itemized deductions to make it worthwhile. In that case save the headache of paperwork and take the standard deduction.

If you do, especially if you are single, keep track of your itemized deductions. Save the bill from the property tax appraiser. Save the 1098 form you receive from your mortgage bank. This form will tell you the mortgage interest you paid. If you donate anything to a charity - get a receipt. You can deduct the value of items you donate as well as the amount of your cash donations. If your itemized deductions from these items are anywhere close to your standard deduction, then it is worth it to explore all of the other more minor itemized deductions to add to your total. If not, take the standard deduction and move on.

The effect of the standard deduction is to make the benefit for the itemized deductions to be zero unless you have a lot of them.

If you are inclined to plan expenses a year in advance, you may want to bundle some of your itemized deductions into the same year in order to have itemized deductions above the standard deduction in one particular year. For example, let's say you are a single homeowner and before charitable contributions you have itemized deductions of about $5000 per year and you donate about $1000 per year to various charities. If you continue doing this, you will get the standard deduction every year. Instead, consider donating $5000 once every five years. In the year with the $5000 charitable donation, you will have itemized deductions of $10,000 instead of the $6300 standard deduction and your tax bill will be lower.

Tip 2: You pay less tax if you group itemized deductions in a particular year rather than spread them evenly.

There's just one more deduction before you are down to your taxable income - it's called "Exemptions". Multiply $4000 by the number of people your income support. If someone else supports you, then your exemption is zero. A married couple with three kids and an elderly parent that lives with them gets six exemptions and a $24,000 exemption deduction. This exemption deduction is in addition to your itemized deductions.

Tip 3: Kids aren't your only deductions. If you provide more than half the support for grandma and can prove it, you can claim her as an exemption too.

Now you're done. After deducting listed deductions, standard (or itemized) deductions, and exemptions from your total income you now know your taxable income. It's common for a married couple to have between $20K and $30K in deductions from total income. That means the first $20K to $30K in total income will not have any income tax at all. There will, however be social security or self-employment tax.

Your taxable income is a very important number. This income amount determines your tax bracket and marginal income tax rate.

If it appears that you will be in a higher tax bracket than you usually are, it is worth it to take steps to lower taxable income this year even if it means raising taxable income in future years. Some easy ways to accomplish this are:

- Increase contributions to retirement accounts (but not Roth).
- Make an extra mortgage payment (if you itemize).
- Purchase a vehicle (if you itemize).
- Pay for optional medical expenses this year (e.g. dental, cosmetic).
- Pay college tuition (yours or someone else's).
- Increase donations to charity (if you itemize).

If it appears that you will be in a lower tax bracket, then increase your income this year. The thought behind that is that you would rather accept income this year when your marginal income tax rate is lower than in a later year where you would pay more taxes on exactly the same income. With enough planning and foresight, you can remain in the same tax bracket for almost your entire life. Some easy ways to accomplish this are:

- Switch retirement contributions to Roth accounts.
- Sell stocks with gains (capital gains tax is 0% for taxable incomes below $70K).
- Rollover an IRA to a Roth IRA - this counts as income.

- Lower contributions to traditional retirement accounts (IRA, 401(k)).
- Wait until next year to make a college tuition payment.
- Wait until next year to donate to charity.
- Don't demand payment for your work until next year (for work done in November and December).

Tip 4: You pay less tax if your income is spread evenly rather than concentrated in a particular year and subject to higher marginal tax rates. This tip is opposite from the tip on spreading expenses.

Finally, after your income tax is calculated, there are a few credits that you may be eligible for that will reduce your tax even further. Credits are the best of all because they directly reduce your taxes rather than your income. Among the most common credits are:

- Dependent care expenses (day camp, babysitter, nanny).
- Education Credits (costs for higher education)
- Child tax credit ($1000 per child) (not available for high earners).
- Earned Income Credit up to $6K for low earners. Not available for families making more than $53K or so.

The effect of all of these credits on top of the deductions will mean that families making less than

$45K or so will not have any income tax payment at all. However they will still be subject to the 7.65% payroll tax.

The goal of these two long chapters is to give you an understanding of how income taxes work. If you have this understanding you will be able to take specific actions in your life that will reduce the tax burden for your family.

Chapter 4 - What Would You Do If You Had $10,000?

$10,000 is starting to be some real money. Way more than $100 or $1000. Again, it would be easy to indulge yourself and spend it all. You could buy a boat or a motorcycle. You could have a great vacation. You could refurnish your house. All of those are nice, for now. A new science called behavioral economics tells us that sooner, rather than later, you'll be used to whatever things you buy and will no longer enjoy them. They'll just be a part of life. Behavioral economics tells us that this will occur within a year. Then, in a few more years, the boat or motorcycle will get old, the memory of your vacation will fade, and your furniture will start to look dated. Your $10K will be gone, and you'll have nothing to show for it.

If you decide to make your money work for you instead of giving it to whoever convinces you to spend your money on something you don't need, you'll be able to enjoy the money for the rest of your life. $10,000 can really get you out of a jam and set you on the right path. Look at your monthly budget. See if there are any ways you can improve your monthly cash flow with the $10K. It is possible you have a credit card or car loan payment you can wipe out by paying it off. There might be a chance that you have to replace an appliance or vehicle that is past its useful life. Replacing the item can free up monthly cash flow going forward. Maybe your cash flow situation gets very tight leading to low balance and overdraft fees from your bank. You can use the $10K can shore up the bank account. Maybe the $10K can pay for you to get a new credential that will get you an increase in pay.

Everyone's financial situation is different. The key, though, to properly handling your first $10K is to make it improve your cash flow. You want to focus on cash flow over everything else because cash flow is forever. Improving cash flow is a virtuous cycle. Once you have consistently positive cash flow, you can use your positive cash flow on items that improve your cash flow even further. Over time, you'll wonder how you ever struggled to make ends meet.

If your cash flow situation is already reasonably good and you can't find a great way to improve your cash flow with your money, then think about your future cash flow. When you first start out your adult life you are hit with a whole bunch of major expenses that you likely don't have the income or savings for. Many people go into debt to pay for these items, crushing their cash flow sometimes for decades. Think about the next five years or so. Are there any major expenses that you are likely to get hit with that you can't pay for with your current income? Among the most common major expenses for young adults are:

- Moving out - moving truck, deposit to electric company, phone company, and furniture.

- Moving in to your first apartment - Many places require "first, last, and security deposit" before they'll give you the keys to your apartment. That could run close to $5K right there.
- A whole new wardrobe for your first "real" job- That "Certified Bikini Inspector" t-shirt isn't going to cut it at the office.
- An engagement ring.
- Your wedding - don't count on Mom and Dad for this. They probably have their own financial issues.
- A new (used) car - You need reliable transportation to get to your new workplace. Don't spend any more than you have to.
- Maybe, if you are really ahead of the game, you see making a down payment on a house within five years.

If you see any of these expenses coming your way in five years or less, stick that $10K in a no fee online high interest savings account and then forget about it. If the bank offers you an ATM or debit card for this account, decline it. You are not to touch this money until you need it. When the big expense comes your way, this $10K will keep you from going into debt. Prior to then, your $10K should give you peace of mind. You know expenses are coming up, and you will be able to pay them with a stroke of the pen. When you set your $10K aside, it should give you

peace of mind today, and positive cash flow
tomorrow.

Chapter 5 - What Would You Do If Your Income Doubled? (It Probably Will Someday)

This is the most fun. It's like the "what if I win the lottery?" question, but a lot more realistic. I know lots of people, including myself, whose income doubled in a short period of time. My income tripled when I graduated from college. It doubled when I left the corporate world to become a consultant. Both of those increases happened when I was under thirty. This is a question that is really worth thinking about because there is a reasonable chance that it could happen to you.

Your thinking on the income doubling question should follow the same line of reasoning as the last chapter. It's all about cash flow. First off, get it in your head that doubling your income usually less than doubles your take home income. It should, though, significantly increase your discretionary spending and savings. Look at a side by side analysis of a single person earning $50K per year who manages to double his income in a short period of time:

	Before Raise	After Raise	Percent Change
Income	50,000	100,000	100%
Social Security Tax	3,825	7,650	100%
Income Tax	5,684	18,184	220%
After Tax Income	**40,491**	**74,166**	**83%**
Necessity Spending	20,000	20,000	0%
Discretionary Spending & Saving	**20,491**	**54,166**	**164%**

The reason for that is simple. Income tax increases much faster than income. That's one of the features of the progressive tax system we have in the USA. A single person earning $50K will more than triple her income taxes when her income doubles. That's because the first dollars are taxed at a much lower rate than your income from a raise.

The reason that discretionary income increases so much is because the price of your necessities doesn't change at all when you get a raise. You still eat the same amount of food every day, live in the same place every day, and spend the same amount of money when you go out with friends. Why wouldn't you? Yesterday, before your raise, you had a good life, why would you change anything? The $34K per year increase in discretionary spending should go directly into savings. This time next year you should have a savings account that has a $34K larger balance.

That never seems to happen. Most people absorb almost all of that increase by increasing their discretionary spending. Starting today, you aren't most people. You don't have to do that. Hold the line on your discretionary spending and increase your savings by as much as possible. That's a lot of savings and will allow you to rapidly build wealth. You'll be able to build a solid emergency fund ($12K to $18K) which is four to six months of expenses depending on the security of your income and the risk level you want to take with your finances.

Once you have your emergency fund in place you can start to think about investing. If your employer has a retirement plan, that is a great place to start. You are eligible to contribute up to $18K to your retirement plan per year. The IRS helps you out on this by not taxing you on this contribution. An $18K contribution to your 401(k) will reduce your tax bill by about $4500 to $5000. So the out of pocket cost of your $18K retirement fund contribution will be about $13K. When you retire, all of that money and the investment gains compounded on top of it comes back to you.

A rule of thumb in the current investing environment is that intelligently invested money doubles approximately every seven to ten years. Your $18K contribution this year will be worth $36K if you are ten years from retirement, $72K if you are twenty years away, $144K if you are thirty years away, and $288K if you are forty years away-- all from a $13K after tax investment. If this isn't a great way to improve your future cash flow without eating into your current lifestyle, I don't know what is.

Chapter 6 - Insurance - What to Buy and When

So what does insurance have to do with financial planning? Insurance is an expense; it's definitely not an investment. The more money a person spends on insurance the less he has available to invest. And usually, you get nothing in return, so what's the point?

Well, in financial planning, we forecast what will happen to your finances if everything goes according to plan. No financial plan will plan for you to die before you fund your child's college education. No financial plan will say that your dog will bite the neighbor's kid and you will get sued. No financial plan will say that your teenage son will accidentally crash his car into another driver and kill all the passengers resulting in a two million dollar judgment against you. No financial plan expects your house to get hit by lightning and burn to the ground. The list goes on and on. Between now and the rest of your life is a long time. Lots of things can happen to your finances and not all of them are good. The average wrongful death judgment is currently about $1.5 million. Thousands of homes are burned to the ground every year. People experience catastrophic (financially and health-wise) events every day. Any one of these disasters would likely crush your finances to such an extent that you could never be able to recover and achieve your financial goals.

Having the right insurance policies in place ensures your financial plan stays on track. While there is a cost to insurance, there is a much bigger benefit. Insurance will increase the likelihood that you will achieve the long term goals of your financial plan and eliminate the possibility of your missing your goals by a catastrophically wide margin. Insurance is not an expense to be deducted from your future net worth, it is a part of your financial plan that ensures your future net worth will come out as planned.

First off, as I stated in the first paragraph of this chapter, insurance is definitely not an investment. Investments are expected to increase in value and retain some value in all but the most serious worst case scenarios. Insurance never has any value unless there is a claim. And, if your insurance portfolio is selected appropriately, there should be very few claims. If you are fortunate, you will be blessed with never having an insurance claim.

That's right, select insurance policies that you believe will never pay a claim. Expenses that you expect to pay can more cheaply be paid from a well stocked emergency fund. You see, insurance is a little bit like playing the numbers in Vegas. Insurance companies predict how many claims there will be and the cost of those claims using troves of historic information on claims and advanced statistical methods. Then they figure out how much they have to charge to pay all of those claims and then add a little more for all of the expenses associated with issuing insurance policies as well as profit. A "little more" is probably an understatement. It costs quite a bit of money to do all the work associated with issuing insurance policies. Typically the insurance premiums paid by policyholders are between 25% and 100% more than the amount the insurance company needs to pay all policyholders' claims. If the cost of a potential insurance claim is small enough to pay for with your emergency fund, you should plan to do so. Using your own funds to pay for these costs will save you the markup that the insurance company charges.

On the other hand, there are some costs that are just too high for your emergency fund to pay for. Think of your target balance for your emergency fund. For me the target balance is about $25K. That's the amount I will pay if I have to buy a new (used) car tomorrow. Some people use a multiple of monthly spending or some other method to determine their emergency fund balance. A key item to remember though is that your insurance policies should pick up where your emergency fund leaves off. So, for me, any financial disaster that can potentially cost more than $25K I am buying insurance no matter what. I am willing to pay the markup in exchange for a guarantee that I will achieve my long term financial plan. Any disaster that will cost me less than $25K, I will pay for out of my emergency fund and avoid paying the insurance company markup.

So in short the key things to consider:

1. If the policy is likely to pay a claim, then you shouldn't buy the insurance. It will be cheaper for you to save your premium payment and pay the claim out of your savings when / if it occurs. Managing the risk that way will allow you to save on the insurance company markup and the hassle of filing a claim. Home maintenance, short-term disability, and some warranty insurance fall into this category.

2. If you can afford to pay the claim out of your savings or other readily available cash and using that cash won't ruin your long term finances, you don't need insurance. Save your money and strengthen your emergency fund. Comprehensive coverage on your car and contents coverage on your personal property fall into that category.

3. If there are no financial consequences to the insured event happening, then you don't need the insurance. Remember, an insurance policy doesn't prevent the insured event from happening, it just pays you if it does. And the insurance company determines premium such that it pays out only 50% to 80% of what the policyholders pay in. An insurance policy is a losing bet that you don't want to make unless the claim payout would be critical to your financial survival in the event of a claim. Life insurance for anyone without financial dependents fall into that category.

Now that I've shared the underlying philosophy of insurance, let me bring it down to the real world.

Homeowners Insurance -- You probably need this. If you have a mortgage, the mortgage company will force you to buy it (you agreed to this when you signed your mortgage documents). What would happen if the insured property were destroyed? Could you survive? For most people, paying to rebuild a home that just burned down would be catastrophically difficult or impossible. Especially since the cost of the mortgage, property tax, and temporary living expense would continue after the property is destroyed. Related to homeowners insurance are insurance for special hazards -- earthquake, flood, hurricane, etc. If you need homeowners insurance, you need insurance for these special hazards as well. The financial catastrophe of paying to rebuild a home doesn't differentiate between a fire and an earthquake. You will need to make sure that the policy limit is high enough to pay to rebuild your house. This amount is usually less than the market value of the house (which includes the land). You might be able to slightly reduce the cost of the policy by increasing deductibles and eliminating optional coverages with low benefits. You should increase deductibles as much as possible as long as they are smaller than the value of your emergency fund.

Other Property Insurance -- You might want this. There are lots of types of property insurance. You can insure your jewelry, art, and other valuable items from disappearance or destruction. What would happen if your jewelry disappeared? Can you live without

33

replacing it? If you can, you don't need the insurance. Do you have enough money saved in your emergency fund to replace it? If you do, skip the insurance and avoid the markup. Only buy the insurance if your answer is no to both of the above questions.

Comprehensive Auto Insurance -- Hopefully you don't need this. Comprehensive auto insurance is just another type of property insurance so the questions in the property insurance section apply. You are almost certain to need to replace your car if it is destroyed, so the question on auto comes down to whether or not you have a car loan or would need a car loan to buy your next car. If you are still dependent on car loans, you need the insurance. If you can pay cash for your next car, you don't need the insurance.

Auto Liability Insurance -- You absolutely need this. It's the law. What you have to decide about auto liability insurance is how high a limit to get. Each state has a minimum requirement. Most states have a $25K / $50K minimum requirement meaning the insurance company will pay a maximum of $25K to each person you injure in an accident and $50K total in payments per accident. Then they walk away. The person you injure in the accident can choose not to accept the insurance company's payment offer and instead sue you in court. If that happens, you are on your own for legal expenses as well as any judgment amount above your policy limit. Medical costs, lost wages, and rehab costs are all very expensive. Even a relatively minor accident where the car accident victim injures his back or neck can result in a judgment over $25K. Major accidents, or accidents resulting in multiple injuries can easily cost in the hundreds of thousands of dollars. The average court settlement for a wrongful death accident is between $1M and $2M. If you are subject to a court judgment, the only alternative to paying the judgment in full is to file for bankruptcy and sign over nearly all of your assets to the car accident victim. Obviously this is catastrophic to anyone with significant savings. A common rule of thumb is to make sure your liability insurance limits are at least as high as your total net worth at risk. When you are just starting out and living paycheck to paycheck it is OK to just take minimum limits. After all your financial status isn't really harmed if you have to file bankruptcy. On the other hand, if you have managed to build a net worth you will need to increase your auto liability limits. The highest liability limit offered by most auto insurers is $250K. If you need more, you will have to buy umbrella insurance. It should be your goal to need this expense!

Umbrella Insurance -- You probably don't need this but hopefully you do. Umbrella insurance covers any and all judgments against you (subject to reasonable exclusions) that aren't covered by other insurance. You can get umbrella policies of up to $5M per occurrence. Most commonly umbrella insurance pays for and defends auto accident claims that are above $250K. But they also cover non-auto related claims such as dog bites, slip and falls, wrongful deaths, and almost any other instance where another person may sue you. O.J. had an umbrella policy that paid out its limits when he lost the wrongful death lawsuit made against him.

Life Insurance -- Maybe you need this, it's complicated. You will definitely be faced with making a decision about life insurance several times in your life. There are many types of life insurance and life insurance salesmen are compensated very well to convince you to buy life insurance. I actually met a "financial planner" who stated "I have never met anyone who doesn't need more life insurance." (He gets paid on commission and is full of crap. He is also very convincing and sells a lot of life insurance).

Two things to know right off the bat that will make your life insurance discussions simpler: 1) It is almost certain that you do not need any type of life insurance except term insurance. While other flavors of life insurance are appropriate in limited situations for high net worth people (assets over $1.5M), those situations are rare and are outside the scope of this chapter. 2) Plenty of people don't even need term insurance.

The question on whether you need life insurance boils down to whether or not your dependents will be able to pay their bills without your paycheck coming in. If you have no dependents, you can skip the life insurance. If you do have dependents who will be inheriting money from you, you will need to calculate whether their income (if any) plus their inheritance can support the lifestyle you want them to have.

Based on these questions there will be different times in your life where you will need life insurance and in different amounts. If you do need insurance your next decision is to determine the amount of insurance you will need and the length of time you will need it (the term). Common reasons to stop needing insurance is when your kids reach financial independence, or when you expect your life savings to be large enough to support your family for the rest of their lives. The shorter the term, the lower your annual insurance premium will be. Before you gain financial independence, you won't need any life insurance because your heirs will need less money to support the family lifestyle after you are gone (dead people don't spend money, so they can be financially dependent on less).

Disability Insurance -- If you need life insurance, you need disability insurance. There is a lot higher chance of becoming disabled than there is of dying. Disability insurance pays you a tax free income from three months after you become disabled until you recover, turn 65, or die. The problem with disability insurance is that you never get a raise while you are disabled and many disability policies require you to work at any job that you are healthy enough to do even if you don't like it. For example a model with burns to her face could be expected to work in the stock room at a grocery store. The disability policy will deduct the grocery store income from the payout. The monthly benefit of the disability policy should be related to the portion of your paycheck that you and your dependents rely on to maintain your lifestyle. You should also make sure there is an inflation rider on the policy so that your benefits can increase with inflation. You can save money by increasing the waiting period from three months to six months provided you have enough emergency fund to cover a full 6 months of living expenses until the disability policy kicks in.

Health Insurance -- Definitely get it. For one thing, the Affordable Care Act says it's the law. Sure, you can decide not to buy it and instead pay the penalty, but to me it's kind of silly to pay something for nothing instead of buying something you almost certainly need. Health insurance checks all of the boxes for a necessary policy. It potentially pays out hundreds of thousands of dollars that you don't have lying around in your emergency fund. These costs are also absolutely necessary for you.

Health insurance provides an added benefit that most other types of insurance do not provide. Medical providers charge people with health insurance much less than they charge people without health insurance. How much less? Well, I can tell you anecdotally that a few years ago my wife needed an appendectomy. The hospital misfiled the paperwork and thought she didn't have any health insurance. The bill came to $38,000. I called the hospital, provided my high deductible insurance policy number, and voila, the bill changed to $6,000. That was under our $10,000 deductible so we had to pay the entire claim. The insurance company paid nothing. However they still saved our family $32,000 in medical costs in one day. That was equal to about seven years in health insurance premiums. Yes, even though my health insurer has never paid a claim in the nine years since I switched to a high deductible insurance policy, the policy has been totally worth it to me.

Assuming your emergency fund is solid, I recommend getting a high deductible insurance policy. You'll save a few hundred dollars per month and can rely on your emergency fund to pay your non-catastrophic medical expenses. The high deductible policy also allows you to contribute to a health savings account and get income tax and investment income tax benefits.

There are a few pitfalls with high deductible policies, though. For one thing, there are a few times when the health insurance fee schedule is higher than what you could negotiate on your own. I have noticed for emergency room visits many insurers negotiate a flat fee. for every emergency room visit no matter how basic the services. I recommend that if you have an ER visit for a minor injury you don't show the insurance card. Wait until you get your medical bills. Then if the total bill adds up to more than the flat fee then you call the billing department and give them your policy number and ask what the adjusted charge is, it might be less. If it is less than the flat fee, just pay the bill, the insurance company probably won't be able to help you.

Dental Insurance - Almost never get that. Dental claims are relatively small. Put the premiums into savings and pay dental expenses as they come up. By avoiding dental insurance you get the added benefit of being able to choose your own dentist and getting preferential treatment because dentists generally prefer to not deal with insurance company paperwork.

Critical Care Insurance -- That's a close call. There are some insurance policies that provide extra coverage for specific illnesses like cancer. Generally I'd prefer to make sure my health insurance policy has reasonable deductibles for all medical issues. Handling the risk that way saves the effort of coordinating care and reimbursement between your health insurance and the critical care insurance.

Travel Health Insurance -- Probably you should get that. These policies provide emergency health insurance coverage if it is required while you are traveling outside the USA. Usually the policy limit and potential expense is $50K to $100K which is large enough to require coverage. It doesn't provide any reimbursement for trip cancellation, hotel deposits, or missed flights.

Travel Cancellation Insurance -- Don't bother. This provides reimbursement if you have an illness that prevents you from taking a trip. If you are ill, you need to get well, that's it.

Pet Insurance -- No way. Medical costs for pets are relatively small. Make sure you can afford to pay for any medical costs your pet might require before you take Spike home from the pound. If you can't afford the medical costs, you can't afford Spike.

Warranty Insurance -- No way. My first rule about insurance is not to buy insurance that you know will have a claim for. Warranty insurance will definitely have a claim. Things break. Deal with it. Pay for the repair out of your savings. without the hassle of filing a claim and hoping the insurer promptly fixes your item.

Credit Card Insurance -- No way. First of all, you shouldn't be carrying a balance, so you shouldn't need the insurance. Secondly, if you do have a credit card balance, you should be figuring out how to pay it off by spending less money. Start with the savings on credit card insurance.

Business Insurance (Errors and Omissions) -- Yes way. If you are in a profession where you can get sued for doing a bad job, you need to buy the insurance. Umbrella policies do not cover these lawsuits. In many cases the person that sues you for doing a bad job will claim that your negligence cost them hundreds of thousands or even millions of dollars. You have to defend these claims even if they are frivolous. Defending a claim like this is difficult and

41

expensive. Your E&O policy will provide you with a lawyer and defend you in this case. Don't expect your business to always shield your personal net worth from a hungry claimant and attorney. They often figure out ways around your business to access your personal net worth.

The beginning of this chapter gave you some principles to guide you in creating the insurance program that is right for you and your finances. The second half of the chapter works to apply those principles to determine whether to buy different insurance products that are commonly offered. Follow these recommendations to keep your financial plan on track at the lowest possible cost.

Chapter 7 - Big Ticket Items - Leaving The Nest, School, Car, House, Wedding, Kids, and Retirement

Big ticket items are an often ignored aspect of personal finance. They aren't really budget items because you can't pay for big ticket items out of your monthly paycheck. They aren't emergencies so the emergency fund concept doesn't work either. Big ticket items need to be addressed on their own.

I define a big ticket item as follows:

> "A reasonably certain expense related to an expected event. The amount of the expense is reasonably well known and larger than total monthly expenses for an ordinary month. The timing of the expense is reasonably well known and at least one year in the future."

You should translate your need for a big ticket purchase to a financial goal. Then, as you should do with any goal setting project, you must set some specifics around your goal to turn it into an effective financial plan. Specifically, you need an achievement date and a dollar amount. For example, you would need to change the vague statement of "I am saving up to pay for my wedding" to a specific goal like "I will save $24,000 before June 1, 2019 so I can pay for my wedding." This specificity delivers focus to you and it also makes creating a "sure thing" financial plan a straight forward algebra problem.

Creating the plan from this goal is simple. However, you should write it down anyway. A possible plan for the above goal is

"Every two weeks, on the day I get paid, I will autodraft $500 from my checking account to a new no-fee savings account I set up for my wedding costs. That will be the only monthly transaction for the savings account."

A simple 41 word plan like the one above embodies all of the characteristics of a big ticket item savings plan.

You need to pay the most important expenses first. That's why the IRS takes out your taxes right away-- because it's that important-- to them.

This plan is also automated. Once you set it up, you don't even have to think about it. In recent years there has been significant research in behavioral science on how to establish good behaviors. These studies have shown that the less conscious effort you have to make to engage in a behavior, the more likely you are to continue. This effect is used often in business and finance. Companies "auto-renew" subscriptions, 401(k) plans auto-enroll employees, and moms put out snack plates of celery, cucumber, and apple slices. Take advantage of this effect in your big ticket saving plan.

The plan is also specific. It requires you to take out $500 a paycheck. $499 is not enough. The specificity means there is no way you can convince yourself you are following the plan when you are not. Weasel words like "I will save as much as possible..." give you too much room to fail.

Finally, you are contributing to a specified bank account that has no fees. The interest rate on the account is irrelevant. At a 1.00% interest rate (that's high for savings accounts) will result in an average of about $10.40 in interest per month for this account. Many banks have monthly fees almost that high. So a bank account with (unnecessary) monthly fees is, at best the same as a no interest account. If you are having trouble finding a no fee bank account, just type "no fee savings account" in your favorite search engine. When you get the ATM / debit card for your no fee savings account, put it in the shredder. You want to make it difficult to withdraw the money.

Lastly, there is the requirement of there being the only one transaction into the account. This requirement prevents you from treating your growing savings account into a slush fund for whatever fun you are looking for at the moment. Your rejection of checks and a debit card helps here also. Remember that Disney movie called "Up" where the couple had a piggy bank for the "adventure of a lifetime", but they kept using a hammer to break the bank for whatever their financial needs were at the moment. The couple never did reach their financial goal even though they saved their whole lives. This couple made the mistake of not really treating the piggy bank like a big ticket account. They treated it as an emergency fund. As a result they always had emergencies and never had their big adventure. They should have gotten rid of all of their hammers so it would be much harder to break the piggy bank.

Some of you may suggest that a person should invest the money in the hopes of having investment gains help pay for the big ticket item. Well, investment gains are not guaranteed. You could actually lose money. Investing your big ticket savings results in your losing control of the amount in your account. Some people subconsciously do that on purpose so they have an avenue of blame if something goes wrong. Don't give yourself that out. Maintain full responsibility and control of your goals. Turn them into concrete plans and achieve them. You'll be happier you did.

Chapter 8 - When to Get Financial Advice

Some people view a relationship with a financial adviser as a status symbol, like a beach house or a new BMW. Those people choose to hire a financial adviser as soon as they can "afford" it, or as soon as their net worth meets the asset requirement of the financial adviser. I think it is more appropriate to view a relationship with a financial adviser like a relationship with your family doctor. You should seek to develop a long-term relationship with a financial adviser so the adviser can get to know you really well and understand the details of your financial situation. Then you should consult with your adviser whenever you need to ensure you are making the best possible decisions about your personal finances. I view the most beneficial relationship you could have with a financial professional is a coaching style relationship. The financial coach is always there when you need education, guidance, or support regarding your financial situation. However, the coach is someone who never seeks to take control of your personal finances. You always retain control. Did I tell you that I am a financial coach?

It is important to periodically check-in with your financial coach. During these check in meetings you should have your coach review your current financial situation. You should also update her on any changes in your personal information that might affect your financial plan.

Possible changes include:

- Changes in job or income expectations.
- Changes in family situation.
- Changes in living arrangements.
- Changes in health or life expectancy.
- Financial windfalls or losses.
- Significant changes in personal expenses.
- Changes in life goals.
- Changes in financial goals.
- Changes in risk tolerance.

As part of this check-in process, your coach will update your financial plan and ensure you are continuing to head towards your financial goals.

In addition to the periodic check in you should seek financial advice whenever you have major financial decisions facing you. The financial coach's fee is usually more than paid for by the improved financial result and peace of mind you get by following the advice of the adviser when you are facing the critical financial decisions of your life.

Important times where a financial coach can help you include:

- When you first begin professional life-- budgeting, insurance decisions, setting up retirement accounts, handling student loan payments efficiently.

- After you build up enough savings where it may be worthwhile to begin investing-- how and where to set up a brokerage account, appropriate investments for your specific financial situation.
- Before you get married-- combining finances, paying for a wedding, changes to insurance and tax situations, updating financial goals.
- When you have children-- changes to insurance and tax situations, updating financial goals, changes in expenses, possible job or home changes.
- Buying your first home-- Getting the right mortgage for you, updating financial plan.
- Selling a home-- tax consequences, how to manage the profits.
- Starting your own business-- Getting financing, budgeting and cash flows of the business, updating your insurance and retirement account needs.
- Selling your own business-- Determining the fair value, managing the changes in your tax and insurance situation, effectively handling the financial windfall, updating your insurance and retirement account needs.
- Early college planning-- If you expect to pay for your children's college, it is important to begin planning early and continuously revisit the plan. College planning includes choosing appropriate investments and investment accounts.

- Late college planning-- Once your child is 3 or 4 years away from college, it's time to begin the effort towards scholarships, financial aid, and college selection. At this time you can also begin to plan for specifics on how your child's college will be paid for.
- Retirement-- As retirement approaches, you can begin to plan for reversing the engine of your financial plan and plan for investment and retirement account withdrawals. You'll have to make decisions about pension distributions, IRA distributions, budgeting during retirement and other items.
- Legacy Planning-- Once you reach retirement age, it is worthwhile to begin making concrete plans about what you want to happen to your money after you are gone. Depending on your situation, you may wish to explore sharing some of your wealth early so you can see the benefit it provides. Effective legacy planning also reduces income taxes and estate taxes.

Chapter 9 - Where to Get Advice

The services that a financial adviser, financial planner, or financial coach is able to provide or willing to provide is one of the most misunderstood aspects of the financial services industry. It is misunderstood by young people and older established people alike. Often people select a financial adviser with the expectation that the adviser will outperform the market. Financial advisers do not outperform the market. The financial adviser community has not demonstrated any success in recommending investments that generate a higher return than simple market index investments. Don't pay a financial adviser if all you want are stock tips. Buy a crystal ball for that.

A financial adviser is not a broker. Yes, there are broker / dealers who call themselves financial advisers. However they are no more financial advisers than your local Ford dealer is a car adviser. Broker / dealers are paid to sell you financial products. Their main sales technique is to advise you that, after performing a thorough analysis of your personal financial situation, they have determined that you absolutely need to purchase the financial product that they have for sale and get a commission on. Don't hire a financial adviser if all you want are mutual funds. You can buy great mutual funds online without paying commission. For example, you can't go wrong with Vanguard. They're the low cost leader and they have index funds that outperform the majority of mutual funds sold through brokers. Even if you find a broker that agrees to "just work on referrals", he's still too expensive. If you have a decent size retirement fund that you invest through a broker, the annual broker's commissions alone can easily run into the five figures. No wonder he is giving you "free" financial advice.

A financial adviser is also not a life insurance salesman. Sure a financial adviser may recommend that you buy life insurance after reviewing your specific financial situation. In almost all cases where life insurance is needed, term life is the way to go. You can buy term life online. There's no complicated forms, and a good financial adviser can even recommend the site to go to and the appropriate policy limit and term length.

So in short, don't go to a broker / dealer, bank, or any financial adviser that you have ever heard of.

The best financial advisers are those that accept a fiduciary duty towards you. A fiduciary duty means that the adviser is looking out for your best interest above everything else. You'd think that all financial advisers do that. They don't. Financial advisers have no such obligation. Many financial advisers, pretty much anybody who sells you a financial product, are only required to recommend "suitable" investments. A suitable investment is an investment type that is appropriate for you. It may or may not be the best choice of that investment. For example, if a large cap mutual fund is suitable for you, a financial adviser following the suitability standard can recommend any large cap mutual fund--even one that underperformed its peers every year for the past ten years or a fund that charges an additional 1.00% management fee. While that may sound egregiously unethical, it actually happens all the time. A substantial percentage of mutual funds sold to retail investors have commission arrangements with financial advisers. And the commissions are paid for straight out of the mutual funds. Yes, the commissions are paid for by you!

So, if you want to hire a financial adviser, you absolutely need a financial adviser that follows the fiduciary standard. Here's how I would go about finding such an adviser. If you want your advisor to make investments on your behalf, you must select a financial services firm that is a Registered Investment Adviser (RIA). An RIA is a firm licensed either with individual states' securities department, or with the Securities and Exchange Commission (SEC) if it is large enough. One of the requirements to become an RIA is the requirement to maintain a fiduciary standard to all clients. Periodically RIAs are audited to verify that they are upholding the fiduciary standard to their clients. So, If you limit your search to RIAs and individuals that work for RIAs, you are sure to be OK.

You can find RIAs by searching for RIAs online. You could also contact the SEC to find all SEC registered

RIAs; Additionally, you can contact the Office of Financial Regulation in the state you reside in.

A financial coach maintains the fiduciary standard towards its clients as well. Unlike an RIA, a financial coach will not make an effort to take control of your investments and finances. A financial coach will review your goals as well as your investment portfolio and then make recommendations to you that will increase the chances you achieve your financial goals. You may follow or ignore those recommendations as you see fit. If you need help following the recommendations, your financial coach will help you with that as well. I am a financial coach. You can find out more about financial coaching services on my website at www.forwardfinancialplanners.com.

There are several networks of financial planners that review the certifications and backgrounds of their members to ensure that they are "quality" financial planners that look out for their clients best interest. The main part of the network's review process of the financial planner is to ensure that the planner has paid the annual membership fee to the network. Many of these networks also verify that their members have a particular level of financial education. While these networks make quality planners easy to find, they won't necessarily deliver a higher quality financial adviser than you could with your own search.

Chapter 10 - Thoughts on Making a Living - You Know Money Is A Factor, So Act Like It

Choosing your job and your career are really important decisions. For your adult life, you spend more than half of your waking hours at work, going to work, talking about work, answering emails about work, etc. So you better be happy with your work. So goes the common wisdom and I agree with that thought.

Some people translate those thoughts into "Choose the job you like most and the money will follow." or the more succinct "Find your passion and follow your bliss." Those are two of the worst pieces of career advice I received as a young adult. Both are 100% untrue and illogical to boot. Just because you enjoy doing something and you are willing to make an effort at it, that doesn't mean you will be paid well, or even paid at all. It also isn't necessarily going to make you happy. A person who comes home from a blissful job to a stack of unpayable bills is going to be unhappy for the rest of the evening. A person who can't afford to pay for the things that help their leisure time be enjoyable isn't going to enjoy the time they spend outside of the workplace. While enjoying your work is important for happiness, enjoying your leisure time is also important to your happiness and that takes money.

My thoughts are that while income shouldn't be the sole factor in your career choice, it should definitely be a factor. The income that should be a factor should be career income, not starting salary. There are some careers where experienced people make double or triple the income of new hires. There are others that have a relatively small income differential for job experience. When thinking about a career or career change, you want to know the long term income potential, not just the starting salary.

The story of my wife's career path has influenced my thoughts on the relationship between income and career choice a great deal. My wife was fortunate enough to have found her passion very early in life-- late high school I believe. She wanted to be a reporter, a journalist. It seems to me she was one of those idealist journalists. She wanted to make a positive difference in the world, expose corruption, and educate the general public.

She did all of the right things to set herself up for a career in journalism. She took the right classes, went to the right college. She selected the best major for her career (journalism, duh), joined the right clubs (school newspaper), got the best internship (local paper), and graduated from college with good grades and great career prospects. Then she interviewed for jobs.

It was only then that she found out how much journalists earned. She was disappointed to find out that she wouldn't be able to afford the lifestyle she desired. She would have to live in a neighborhood she wasn't comfortable with. After years of preparation, she let go of her plan to be a journalist and chose an alternate career path with better income prospects. I view this story as a cautionary tale of what could go wrong if you ignore income when choosing your career path.

Now the fact that journalism turned out to be the wrong career path for my wife does not mean it is the wrong career path for everyone. Some people might find that they are able to be happy on that income. Some people may have other sources of funds that allow them to accept a lower income than they otherwise would. Some people may find a path to creating a higher income in that field than my wife did.

The point of that story is that the income of a career path is an important factor in choosing that career path.

I have another friend who selected his career based on only one factor- starting salary. He gave no thought to whether he would enjoy his career or how his career would progress over the years. Ten years later, he was out. He found an entirely new career that he enjoys just as much. However, his new career had a much higher upside potential. It was a real win for him to switch careers. He did switch and he did stick with it. He wishes he made the switch sooner.

When making a career choice, consider your potential income both when you start and years down the road. Only after you have that information can you make an intelligent career choice.

Then once you've made your career choice, make sure there will be a job available to start your career. Now it's time to start working backwards. Look at the job requirements. Make sure you are on the correct path to have those requirements. Find somebody with the career that you want. Talk to them and show them your resume. Ask if that resume is good enough to get an entry level job. If not, ask what you need to do to get your resume at the top of the interview pile. Now figure out how to do that. Figure out how much time it will take and figure out how much it will cost.

Hooray! You've reduced another life decision to a cost benefit analysis. The costs are time, money, and effort. Effort may be in the form of doing grunt work that may not be fun, or other forms of "paying your dues" that are common for people starting out in a new career. The benefits are income and the satisfaction generated from your career (this could be negative if you dislike your job). While working your way through the process of taking a life decision and turning it into a cost benefit analysis won't guarantee that you will make the right choice. However does guarantee that you will actually gather all the facts and think things through completely before making your career choice. That goes a long way.

Chapter 11 - What is Your Money Mission / What Does Money Mean for You?

Shortly after you have figured out how to make ends meet, it's worthwhile to start to think what you want your money to do for you over the course of your life. Sure, you want your money to feed, clothe you, and keep you from living under a bridge. Everyone wants that. What next? What do you want your money to do for you after you've handled those basic needs?

Some people want to grow their net worth so they can live an increasingly large lifestyle. Others want to save as much money as possible so they can retire early and never have to take orders from anyone again (Wall Street types call that f*** you money). Some would prefer to spend as much money as possible in the present once they have an emergency fund covered. The list goes on and on.

Anyway, once the emergency fund is covered, you need to start thinking about what you want your money to do for you now and in the future. If you don't have that conversation with yourself, you won't be able to decide what you should be doing with your money now, and nobody (not even you) will be able to generate a financial plan for your future. You'll be like the guy in the mutual fund commercial who tells his friend that he needs to save "a gazillion dollars" and whenever he gets extra money he just throws money at his retirement. That's a guy without a plan, and he's also a guy who will never feel financially secure. Don't be that guy.

It is ingrained in our culture that we must save money "to take care of the future". Most people agree that it is important to save. Many try to make this need more concrete by translating that into a goal to save for retirement. However, even the "save for retirement" goal is pretty vague. The cost of retirement is influenced by the age you wish to retire at, the amount you wish to spend during retirement, and the income you expect to earn during retirement. You need to get those two items down to have a shot at an intelligent retirement savings plan.

Another part of your money mission is your decision on how to get to retirement. Some may wish for the emotional comfort of getting there as soon as possible, while others would like to spend as much money as possible while they are young even if it requires future sacrifices when they are older.

The emotional aspect of what money and wealth mean to you is critical to developing your money mission. For example, in my life having a comfortable savings amount increases my sense of freedom and personal security I seek the freedom not to take orders, and the personal security of knowing that I'll always have money for any emergency that comes my way. For much of my life my financial plan has involved saving all of my money after I've paid for food, clothing, and shelter. For me, managing finances has been mainly about maximizing investment returns and calculating how much more money I need to save in order to be able to maintain my lifestyle without earning an income. Others prefer to take the approach of figuring out how much money they "should" save per month.

Some people view wealth as a way to keep score and validate their own sense of worth. Some people feel that saving money is a waste and spend it as soon as they get it-- often on things that everyone would agree are a waste of money. The point is that everyone has different views around money and wealth. The views that you have should influence your financial plan. Make sure your views on money and wealth are compatible with your financial plan.

Chapter 12 - When You Have to Spend More Than You Earn

I've spent this whole book telling you that you must spend less than you earn. You must have money left over to put in an emergency fund or retirement savings. And yes, that's usually true. However there are times in your life when you must spend more than you earn. If you've been managing your money properly, you'll probably be able to access your additional spending needs from your savings.

Spending more than you earn is the most common way you can get yourself on the road to financial ruin so taking this step is not something to be taken lightly. You need to set some ground rules with yourself in order to protect yourself from the potential financial ruin.

Rule #1:   Have a plan, a mini financial plan, just for this important period in your life.

Rule #2:   Know when the "spending more than you earn" will stop. If you don't know when it will stop, then it won't and you definitely should drop your plan to spend more than you earn.

Rule #3:   Play out two scenarios: One for the time period from when you begin spending more than you earn until one year after you stop; the second scenario is for the same time period except you don't spend more than you earn. Only spend more than you earn now if it is the scenario where you end up happier and better off one year after you are done spending more than you earn.

You don't need any professional help creating the mini financial plan required by Rule #1. You do need to write it down, though. It will need some vivid details in it in order for you to be able to follow rules #2 and #3. Answer these questions for yourself:

- How much money do you need above your earnings?
- For how long will you be spending more than you are earning?
- When do you need it?
- Where are you going to get it?
- What are you going to do with it?
- When will you be able to replenish the savings drawdown and / or repay the loan?

Once you write it down, read it. Is it believable? Is it detailed enough for your future self to be able to follow the plan? Once the plan meets your standards, keep it handy and review it regularly. You'll want to review it to make sure you are following it, and also identify if you need to change the plan based on new information. There's a good chance you'll need to change the plan. That's OK... provided that the revised plan answers all of the above questions also. If your revised plan doesn't have an end date for your excess spending, watch out! It's the first sign that you are becoming addicted to spending beyond your means. Time to rein it in, or even cut yourself off from excess spending. Always have an end date for spending beyond your means. Because if you don't have an end date, one will be provided to you by the banks. And the banks' end date will come up without warning at the least convenient time. Stay in control of your finances and follow your plan.

Stay the course and you'll get through the tough times eventually. If you don't review your plan, you will forget what it really says and you'll stop following it. You'll move from the category "A man with a plan" to the category "A guy who spends beyond his means". You definitely don't want that.

Example:
Mary is writing a book about her experience in the military. Once she started she realized that she doesn't have enough time to write because of her second job. She decides to quit the second job at least temporarily so she can complete the book. Without the income from her second job she'll be spending more than she earns. She has some savings, and she doesn't want to get herself in financial trouble. She decides to create a mini plan for herself to keep herself focused, on track, and out of financial trouble. Here's the mini-plan she created.

How much money do you need above your earnings?

The book will take six months to write. There is a schedule to keep on track. The second job has been bringing in $20K per year. So $10K should cover the financial need.

For how long will you be spending more than you are earning?

Six months - the time it takes to write the book. Beginning July 1, and ending December 31.

When do you need it?

Spread out over the entire 6 month period--$10K / 26 weeks = $384 per week.

Where are you going to get it?

There is $20K in my emergency fund. I'll use $10K.

What are you going to do with it?

Support living expenses and pay all credit card bills on time.

When will you be able to replenish the savings drawdown and / or repay the loan?

Six months after returning to the second job -- July 1 of next year.

This is an excellent plan. Following it will keep her out of trouble. It is a concrete plan as to amounts, duration of excess spending, and time to payback. She is also aware that things may not work out as well as hoped and Mary has a path to financial recovery no matter the outcome of her book. I would be comfortable advising Mary to go for it.

Example 2

Harold and Judy want to have a baby. They want Judy to stay home as a full time mom for a while. Judy's job currently pays $50K per year ($34K take home). They currently save $10K per year. Harold's job is secure and they don't want to change their lifestyle. They create a mini plan to see if they can reasonably spend more than they earn for this important time in their lives.

How much money do you need above your earnings?

> About $24K per year ($34K lost take home pay minus $10K savings).

For how long will you be spending more than you are earning?

> For a while-- Until Judy is ready to return to work.

When do you need it?

> Beginning on Judy's last day of work until she returns.

Where are you going to get it?

> There is $25K in the emergency fund. There is equity in their home and Harold might get some raises.

What are you going to do with it?

> Support living expenses and pay all credit card bills on time.

When will you be able to replenish the savings drawdown and / or repay the loan?

> After Judy returns to work.

This is a terrible plan. Having a baby is an important milestone in life. Harold and Judy need to know how they are going to pay for the additional costs. Right now they have just vague hopes and dreams. The only thing on the plan that is anywhere close to concrete is how much they want their excess spending to be ($24K/yr). They have no timeframe as to how long the deficit spending will last, they have no idea how they are going to get the money, and they have no idea how they are going to pay it back. The plan has got to change.

Of course they are going to have a baby. Nobody lets finances get in the way of starting a family. However, they should think more deeply about their finances. They probably have to commit to reducing their personal expenses, at least initially. Their spending habits will deplete a $25K nest egg pretty quick. As Harold gets the raises he expects, they can gradually increase their lifestyle again. Another important change to their mini financial plan is to put a date on ending the deficit spending. That date might be when the baby turns three or five. At that time Judy can commit to earning an income again. Their financial plan could require them to begin spending within their means by that time. Their spending will be less than Harold's income plus raises plus Judy's part time income.

These changes are a significant improvement to the financial plan. It sets a hard date for the excess spending to end (required by Rule #2); it also allows H & J to know with certainty where they are going to get the money they will need. Their initial financial plan completely glosses over that section.

So spend less than you earn, except when you don't. But be sure to have a plan to get back in the black if you must spend more than you earn.

Chapter 13 - Credit Cards vs. Debit Cards (vs. Lines of Credit)

You are not going to believe this. Absolutely I use credit cards. I use them as much as possible. I think they are great-- provided that you follow a few rules I outline in this chapter.

Debit cards... I hate them. I put them in the shredder when I get a "free" debit card from the bank "for my convenience". I'll explain why in this chapter.

So, how does a financial coach who hates debt, believes in spending less than you earn, and insists that you don't buy something you don't have the money for justify credit card use? Easy. I take advantage of their features, and avoid their costs.

The first step in making sure that credit cards are a healthy ingredient to your overall financial behavior is the selection of your credit card portfolio. No need to diversify here. You should be using only one credit card. This card is your primary card. Having lots of credit cards just creates additional hassle. One credit card equals one bill equals one call for a replacement card if your wallet is stolen. Each month you should be getting only one credit card bill.

Only one person should be able to charge on your card, and that person is you. When you get your credit card bill, you own it. Those are your purchases. You have to pay the bill alone. Knowing that the bill is yours and yours alone allows you to keep more on top of your purchases and delivers much more of a sense of responsibility towards paying your credit card bill. You can't blame a big credit card bill on your spouse or girlfriend. If you want to help your spouse / girlfriend with their credit card bill, go ahead. But only after you've paid your own bill. If you can't afford to pay the girlfriend's credit card bill, then maybe you can't afford the girlfriend.

Now get a second credit card. This is your backup. The only time you will ever use this card is if your primary card doesn't work for some reason. Maybe somebody stole your card #. Maybe somebody charged up your card and it will take a few days to get things straightened out. Maybe the magnetic stripe doesn't work anymore and your replacement card won't come in the mail for a few days. Whatever the reason, you need a backup credit card, just like you need a backup set of keys. Keep the backup card in the back of your wallet where you can't even see it.

Once you get the issue with your primary card resolved, go online. Pay the balance in full to your backup card. Then put the backup card in the back of your wallet until you need it again. You probably will end up using your backup card somewhere between zero and ten days per year.

Most people need only a primary and backup. If you own your own business that is incorporated and has tax deductible expenses, you might want a business card just to keep business expenses separate from personal expenses. Again, pay the balance in full every month. Use your business bank account.

Racking my brain here, I can't think of a legitimate need for a fourth credit card. If you become wealthy and you can support monthly expenses higher than your credit card limit, just call the company and get the limit raised. If you have multiple businesses, you probably should have a bookkeeper keeping track of business expenses; you won't need a credit card's help.

And if you max out your primary card and can't get a higher credit limit? That means you spent so much in one month that not even the credit card company thinks you should be spending more. If this happens, definitely don't get another card. Pay off the maxed out card promptly and figure out how to not let that happen again.

So, now you've decided how many credit cards you need (two or three), you need to select them. As much as I want to help the little(r) guy, there's only two card companies that can work in this plan - Visa and MasterCard. They are the only two that are accepted everywhere.

Next, you have to decide the features you are looking for on your card. You require your card to have no annual fee-- why would you pay a fee for something when you don't have to? Third, you have to decide what features you are focusing on with your card. Credit card companies tout lots of different features--

low interest, free balance transfers, rewards, late fee forgiveness... the list goes on. Well, since you pay your balance off every month, it's simple to narrow down the features you are focusing on. For most people managing their credit card usage properly, only one feature will matter-- rewards.

In the old days when I was getting my first credit card, there was exactly one credit card with rewards (Discover) and it had exactly one very simple rewards program-- "Up to 1% cash back on every purchase." Now there are lots of competing complicated rewards programs - Disney dollars, airline miles, special rewards for gas or purchases at the mall. Some of these programs do indeed sound enticing. Most rewards programs, though have one or two problems. Some require you to buy only from certain stores to get the rewards or they require you to use the rewards only at certain stores. In my experience, the stores attached to the rewards are usually overpriced stores (like Disney, or the Mall). I require any credit card company that wants to do business with me to offer no strings attached cash on every purchase, and I think you should too. After all, your goal with credit cards should be to use them to make your personal finances less complicated and costly.

Now, every year, when you get your cash back check from your credit card company, you can take that money to help you top off your emergency fund. That's the way to effectively use credit cards in your personal finances.

Debit Cards

Debit cards offer the same primary feature as credit cards- they allow you to buy things without cash or a checkbook. Other than that, debit cards are a whole different animal.

Unlike credit cards, which don't interact with your finances until the end of the month in the form of a bill, debit cards are attached to your bank account and can draw money out of your bank account at will. Usually, banks will set up overdraft protection on your debit card for your convenience. At one very large bank in America (with a similar sounding name) here's how overdraft protection works: 1) They sign you up "for your convenience"; 2) if your balance starts to drop dangerously low, they don't tell you "for your convenience"; 3) if you try to buy something that costs more than you have in your bank account, they don't tell you about the problem "for your convenience"; 4) instead they allow you to spend money that you don't have "for your convenience"; 5) there is a fee, of course, for this free loan. For your convenience, it is a flat fee that they tally for you and do not reveal to you until a later time; 6) well actually the loan isn't free. They charge interest-- about the same as a high interest credit card-- for your convenience; 7) They don't tell you about the interest charges now, they wait until later for that too-- for your convenience; 8) Eventually, when your next paycheck deposits, they immediately use you paycheck to pay all of the charges, interest and fees for your convenience. If the paycheck isn't enough, your bank balance will remain at $0, even after payday.

Debit cards also generally have a "no questions asked" policy towards purchases. If your debit card registers a $500 IPad purchase from Croatia, they will deduct the purchase price directly from your bank account. What does the bank care if the transaction seems a bit fishy. They are getting paid. If you notify the bank of fraudulent purchases on your debit card, they will do a prompt investigation. The process isn't very convenient, though. They wait until they decide that the Croatia IPad purchase is fraudulent before the bank returns your money to you.

As for rewards for debit card purchases - there are none at this particular bank - that's not convenient -- for the bank.

So for me, debit cards are about as convenient as a punch in the face. I'll stick with a credit card.

Chapter 14 - Banking for Grownups

The prior chapters talk about the individual components of personal banking. You've got a checking account (no fee), an emergency fund (high interest online account), a few credit cards (no fee rewards cards), and you've skipped the savings account (1% interest per year isn't worth the hassle). Now here's how I recommend you put them all together.

The first thing you need to do when you are ready to be a grownup in your banking life is to set up your paycheck with direct deposit to your own checking account. Even if your financial life is intertwined with that of your significant other, you should still have your own individual bank account. Having a bank account not shared with anyone else forces you to take ownership of everything that goes on inside it. It also makes it easier to keep an approximate running total and verify that all transactions are legitimate. The same goes for credit cards.

Many banks waive minimum balance fees and provide other small perks if you have direct deposit. Even if your bank isn't rewarding direct deposit, do it anyway. Direct deposit is just a good idea. As a matter of fact make sure all the money you receive -- paychecks, freelance income, gifts, etc. -- lands in your primary checking account.

The bill pay feature contained in every online checking account is the greatest time and expense saver in personal finance. Take advantage of what it can do for you. All your regular monthly bills should have automatic payments coming from bill pay. It goes without saying that your rent / mortgage payment should be coming from bill pay, it's the same amount due to the same person on the same day of the month. That's what bill pay was designed for.

Even if the amount of some bills change every month (e.g credit card and electric), you can still use bill pay for them. Take a look at your past five or ten bills. Figure out the average monthly payment. Add 10% or 20% to the average, and select that amount for bill pay. For months when you pay more than the bill amount, you'll get a credit on your account. The credit will get used up in other months when you pay less. Every six to twelve months, take a look at your bills again and see if you need to make an adjustment to your bill pay amount. Other than that, once you set up bill pay, you never have to pay these bills again.

You should pay a little more attention to your credit card than to your other bills. Credit card bills can be very variable and the interest charges are exorbitant if you don't pay off your credit card bill each month. One month you may go on vacation and spend $3000, while in another month you may not use your credit card for anything except $200 in groceries. You definitely want to review your bill each month and make sure all the purchases are yours. You also want to make a second payment to your credit card as a "one-time payment" to cover any shortfall. Credit card interest charges and late fees are exorbitant, and there's no reason you should be paying them. Your monthly bill pay to your credit card guarantees that you'll avoid late fees. Your one-time payment allows you to avoid interest charges.

Now that you've done the heavy lifting of setting up recurring bill payments for all of your bills, you've done most of the work in creating a monthly budget for yourself. Take your income and subtract all of the monthly recurring payments you set up. That difference is your monthly surplus. It is available for non-recurring payments such as checks you write, ATM withdrawals, and emergency fund contributions.

Now you have enough information to set up your last recurring payment-- your emergency fund payment. If you remember from my chapter on emergency funds, the emergency fund should be set up at another bank where it is a little bit difficult for you to access your money. Decide on the portion of your monthly surplus that can be deposited in your emergency fund, and set up an automatic payment for that amount. You want money going to your emergency fund every month, no matter what. This system accomplishes that.

In six months or so you should revisit all the bills you put on auto pay. You want to revisit for two reasons: 1) to see if you need to change the auto pay amount going forward; and 2) if you have a balance credit (I suggested that you auto pay 10 to 20% above your average bill), then you may be able to cancel your auto pay next month and let your balance credit pay the bill.

The personal finance system described above has several great benefits once it is set up. First, it's a great time saver. Your bill paying time will drop from an hour a month to one to two hours every year! Second, it forces you to grow your emergency fund and turns "emergencies" into regular expenses. Third, it guarantees you will never get hit with a late charge again, preserving your credit rating and saving you $100 - $200 per year. Fourth, it inherently creates a budget for you. Saving on stamps and envelopes are just a bonus.

Chapter 15 - Can You Afford It?

What a dumb question. Actually not dumb, irrelevant. I went to a Yankee game with my son yesterday. He wanted a Yankee T-shirt which I said he could buy with his own money. Stadium prices for the t-shirt were $40 plus tax. Can I afford it? Yes, of course. I had more than $40 in my wallet, and certainly my net worth is more than $40. Can he afford it? Also yes. I offered to lend him the money, and he has more than that in his savings account to pay me back.

Everything that has a price tag less than your net worth is something you can afford. "Can I afford it?" is a question that spenders ask themselves because you can almost always answer affirmatively to that question. Spenders use that question to justify purchases they shouldn't really make. People who manage their money intelligently don't ask that question. Instead they ask "Is it worth it?". The question of worth or value requires a comparison. Sometimes you have more than one comparison. This occurs when you are choosing to purchase one of many items available. That's what I call the kid in the candy store approach-- You've already decided to spend the money, you just need to decide what combination of items delivers the most value to you. That's the easiest kind of spending decision because you have concrete things to choose from.

Often, there is only one comparison- you can compare making the purchase with saving the money (or paying down debt). Unfortunately saving money is quite an abstract concept. You can't see, feel, or touch the savings. It's hard to envision the pleasure of saving money. That's why, for most of us, saving money loses the contest with spending money when something we want is dangling right in front of us.

It requires a little up front work to give "saving money" a fighting chance when compared to a potential impulse purchase staring you in the face. First, turn saving money into a concrete goal with a pleasurable outcome. For example, saving money might become "saving money for a new car next year". That's a good start.

Still, next year is kind of far off, so the new car is still kind of abstract. In my experience, any goal over a month out is really too far away for my brain to appreciate, and financial goals are no exception. I recommend revising your goal further to "saving $1000 this month so I can get a new car." Notice what I did there. The goal is now 1) concrete; 2) short-term; and 3) doable. The new goal also has dire consequences if it isn't met. The implication of the wording is that if you don't save $1000 this month, you can't get a new car. Keep that imagery in your head. Do you really want that junky souvenir from Yankee Stadium, or a new car? Now that's a comparison that saving money can win.

In my perspective, if you have credit card debt, you can't afford anything. You should be buying only necessities(food, clothing, shelter) until you've paid off all outstanding consumer debt. If you are over 30, you can't afford anything if you don't have a solid three to six month emergency fund. If you have a major (more than two months income) mandatory purchase that is more than 10% of your income between now and the expected purchase date and you don't know where the money is coming from then you also can't afford anything.

For example, If you make $4,000 per month, and you know you'll need $20,000 (that you currently don't have) to buy your next car in a year or two, then you can't afford anything. Here's the math:

$20,000 = 5 months income (5 x $4,000 = $20,000).

10% of income times 12 to 24 months = 1.2 to 2.4 months' income. You won't be able to afford the new car that costs 5 months income soon enough.

Or, if you feel like you want to be able to afford some of life's little luxuries in the short-term, you may wish to let go of your plan to get a $20,000 car and plan on getting a $10,000 car. If you do, the math changes as follows:

$10,000 = 2.5 months income;

10 x 2.5 months income = 25 months.

If you are willing to hold on to your current car for 25 more months, you've got a plan to buy a new car. Of course you still should be making the "can I afford it" comparison on all your purchases with the goal of "saving $400 this month so I can get a new car".

Chapter 16 - Can you Afford Not to Buy it?

Some money moves you can't afford not to do. If you avoid these expenses now, it'll cost you much more later. Paying taxes is an obvious one that comes to mind. You can pay your taxes now or you can pay taxes, penalties, interest, audit fees, and possibly court costs later. You definitely can't afford not to pay your taxes when they are due.

Here are some more obvious ones:

- Tune up your car.
- Replace your old air conditioner that still works.
- Increase your retirement account contribution.
- Pay for financial advice (maybe).
- Buy a durable pair of shoes that will last 10 years instead of a cheap pair.
- Buy insurance.

The commonality with all of the things that you can't afford not to do is that not doing them forces you to spend more money at some time in the future. Sure, spending money that you don't have or money that you do have but desire to save can feel like an avoidable pain. However, sometimes an upfront expense now can save larger expenses later. Rather than analyze specific examples, this chapter discusses some items to consider when deciding whether you can afford not to do something.

Buy Durability. Durable items, that is items that have the durability to last significantly longer than their cheaper alternatives are often worth it. Some appliances, shoes, clothes, and furniture fall into this category. For example, quality furniture can last for generations, while furniture you purchase at a big box store and assemble yourself probably won't last as long as the manager of your favorite baseball team.

It is almost never worth it to pay for durability for kids items. Kids have a very financially inefficient habit of growing out of things and interests. They get bigger and grow out of their clothes before they wear them out. They grow into and out of hobbies much more quickly than adults do. Buying durable kids items is a waste. Actually, it's counterproductive. I'd rather have kids items break, wear out, or turn to junk. It makes the decision on whether to throw them out so much easier.

Durable electronics are also pointless. In my entire life, I don't think I have ever repaired any electronics. By the time something breaks, it's ready to be replaced with the next technological leap.

Don't Confuse Status with Durability or Quality. They are absolutely not the same. Often they aren't even related. "You get what you pay for..." (always said or heard in mother's condescending tone) is one of the biggest piles of baloney in personal finance. It's a myth created by sellers of overpriced brands in order to bamboozle people into transferring more of their earnings to the sellers.

The myth is then perpetuated by the bamboozled people to make them feel like they were incredibly intelligent (and smarter than you) for overpaying for their purchases. The condescending tone, while optional, has the added bonus to some of attempting to make you feel stupid. I paid nothing for my wife and son and virtually all of the greatest memories in my life. When I hear "you get what you pay for," I think "you are a bozo". Sometimes I even say it if the person is condescending enough.

An item or brand has status when the general public blindly believes it is "better" than its competitors without any evidence. If someone is trying to sell you a product that is more expensive than its competitors and they can't explain to you what makes their product better and justify the price difference, then they are trying to sell you on status. Of course, if the seller justifies a price differential with the "you get what you paid for..." line, then status is all he is selling. You need to run away from this guy.

The only value that status items may have for you is that it gives you the ability to brag. Not worth it to me. Besides, when I see people flash status items around, I think of them as insecure, not enviable.

Buy Things That Will Increase Your Income. If you are self employed there are probably several things in this category. Marketing and advertising are two things that come to mind right away for businesses. Often marketing generates far more in gross profit than its expense. Can you really afford not to advertise if you can't get customers without it? People in traditional jobs may have the opportunity to buy things that free up their time and enable them to work longer hours and earn more money. Items in that category include lawn service, cleaning service, babysitting, dog walking, etc.) The cost of express mailing packages is often worthwhile compared to the time out of the office you'd have to spend hand delivering it.

Buy Things that Will Decrease Your Expenses.
Replacing inefficient appliances is at the top of the list for me. Refrigerators and air conditioners are continuously being improved. Over the past twenty years air conditioner efficiency has almost tripled. In all but the coldest climates replacing a twenty year old air conditioner is something you can't afford not to do. And that's true even if the air conditioner is working fine. Refrigerators and heating units have the same sorts of efficiency considerations. Sure, you could avoid paying for a new $4,000 A/C by keeping or repairing the twenty year old A/C with little or no cost today. But then, if you buy the A/C and live in a hot climate, you may save $200 a month on your electric bill. In two years your savings will exceed your cost. Every year afterward, your savings will increase by $2,400. Now that's a purchase you can't afford not to make. Refrigerators and heating systems have the same sort of efficiency issues.

Chapter 17 - When Financial Disaster Strikes

Your first line of defense against financial disaster is your emergency fund. Hopefully your financial disaster can be paid off by your emergency fund. Calm yourself down, write a check, and the financial part of your emergency is behind you. Once you dust yourself off, commit to rebuilding your emergency fund. I recommend you develop a plan that rebuilds your emergency fund in no less than three years. I don't think you'll need too much convincing to rebuild your emergency fund right after it saved your butt.

But what if your disaster is bigger than your emergency fund? What if your disaster is a lot bigger? That's what insurance is for. Before disaster strikes, you need to make sure you are covered.

You have car insurance, you have property insurance, maybe you even have some boat insurance. So you're all set, right? Yup, you're all set, unless...

When you are thinking about insurance, there should never be an "unless..."

Unless you are sued.

My other insurance policies have liability coverage you say. You're all set.

What if you are sued for a lot of money? Auto liability insurance limits generally don't go above $250K,

Standard property policies have liability coverage of $300K or less.

What if you are sued for more?

I would never do something so negligent. I'll win in court you say. No problem.

There's still a problem. If you are sued, your insurance company can write a check for your policy limit and walk away. Your insurance company has no further obligation to you. If the plaintiff says "No, $250K is not enough for me. I don't accept that settlement offer," you are on your own. You need to personally secure a defense attorney. Count on about $200K for the lawyers if it goes to trial. If you decide a higher settlement offer is appropriate, you need to add your own money (a lot of money).

Well, $250K is high enough, isn't it?

Sure, it's high enough, unless... What if a person dies or is permanently injured as a result of an accident that is your fault? Half of the wrongful death cases that go to trial and are won by the plaintiff result in a verdict of more than $1.5 million. That's not the kind of money most people have lying around.

Yeah, that's an awfully rare worst case scenario. I'll just declare bankruptcy. Donald Trump did it four times and it worked out for him.

Yup, and you're no Donald Trump. Declare bankruptcy and say "Bye" to your business, your life savings, your house (unless in Florida), your IRA (unless in Florida), and almost everything you have of financial value. If you have a high paying job, a "clean slate" Chapter 7 bankruptcy won't be an option. The plaintiff can force a Chapter 13 bankruptcy and make you agree to a payment plan from your future income.

If you have managed to acquire some wealth and / or a high paying job, everything you've worked for your whole life can come crashing down in a moment.

Umbrella insurance takes care of this problem. And now I know why umbrella insurance is the most neglected insurance policy. It took four hundred words to explain why this insurance is necessary. Compare that to explaining why you need other types of insurance. I can explain the need for property, auto, and life insurance in one Twitter post: "What if your house burns down, what if you get in a car crash, what if you die?"

Umbrella insurance is insurance that picks up where other insurances leave off. The smallest umbrella policy starts at $1M of coverage, and many umbrella insurers will go up to $5M without too much of a fuss. Umbrella insurance is offered by most insurers that sell property and auto insurance. The umbrella insurer will require you commit to maintaining your underlying property and auto policies. They do that because the umbrella policy is structured to come into play only after your property and auto policy have walked away.

If you had an umbrella policy, the lawsuit against you would play out like this:

Once the plaintiff rejects your settlement offer and your insurance company walks away, the umbrella insurer steps in and says "I'm here to help."

In the event of an "average" wrongful death case, the umbrella insurer might offer its $1M policy limit. The plaintiff will be a lot less likely to say no to $1M than he would be to $250K. A $1M check today is usually more attractive than going through the time (often years) and expense (plaintiff attorneys need to eat), and risk (the plaintiff may lose) to get $1.5M (or maybe even less than $1M).

The plaintiff will probably accept the settlement. The case will be over. Your stress will be gone. Your financial future will be secure. And you'll avoid a bankruptcy unlike Donald Trump. You're no Donald Trump.

Umbrella insurance policies usually cost a few hundred dollars per year, and are well worth the peace of mind. Unless... you want to be like Donald Trump.

Chapter 18 - Paying for Services and Spending your Time Effectively

Time is money, after all. When you can spend a little bit of money to free up a lot of time, you have made yourself a great trade. There are several times when it is smartest to shut up and pay for services rather than look for ways around it.

- When you can free up a big block of time for relatively little cost.
- When you can earn more money during the time you would be spending doing the work you paid for.
- When the services allow you to save more money.
- When the services allow you to earn more.
- When the services a professional provides is so much better than what you can do.
- When it provides an insurance policy.

An important input into this decision is how much you value your time. You may think of it as your hourly rate of earnings at work. That would be appropriate if you are considering spending money to increase work time (or avoid lost work time). You may think of your time as more valuable than your hourly rate at work. That would be appropriate if the time you are buying is especially valuable such as extra time with your family if you've been working a lot, or an additional hour of vacation; a higher number would also be valuable if it helps you avoid parts of your life that are especially unenjoyable-- like cleaning or attending the ballet (for me). In other situations it may not be worth very much at all. These situations include times when you are unemployed or a Saturday afternoon when you have nothing to do anyway. The point here is that there is no one dollar amount that equates to an hour of time. The relative value of time and dollars go up and down-- just like any other investment.

Spend the money when you can free up a big block of time for relatively little cost.

This one is relatively straightforward and easiest to analyze. Home improvement tasks are the first thing that comes to my mind for this category. My wife and I decided to paint the inside of our house a few years ago. That's not too hard, I painted the dorms in college, I thought. We lost three long weekends of our lives. So the proper way to weigh the "do-it-yourself" option. is to decide what a free weekend is worth to my family and multiply by three. If that's more than the cost of the painters, then go ahead and pay.

Spend the money when you can earn more money during the time you would be spending performing the services you paid for.

This one is for very busy people that have every minute of their day allocated. Usually they have very demanding jobs where they work as many hours a week as possible. For them, an extra hour of personal time means a lost hour of wages. These people should consider paying for services if the services cost less than what you can earn during that time.

If the services are for your business, you can compare the cost of services to your gross income. However, if the services are not tax deductible services the proper comparison is to your net income. Why net income? You pay for services in your personal life with net income-- income after taxes, work expenses, and social security taxes.

The effect of this differential is that you will end up being more willing to pay for services that help your business than for your personal life. You may pay for office cleaning, but not for housekeeping as an example.

Spend the money on services when the services allow you to save more money.

Paying for experts falls into this category. A tax preparer can potentially save you thousands of dollars by maximizing your deductions and identifying tax efficient financial moves that can potentially reduce your taxes in future years. A financial coach may also be able to save you a great deal by identifying cost efficient investments and retirement plans. A financial coach who can reduce your investment expenses on your portfolio by 1% per year will save a retiree with a $1M investment portfolio $10K per year. If the financial coach's fees are less than $10K per year, the advice will pay for itself. My financial coaching website, www.forwardfinancialplanners.com has several articles discussing ways financial coaches save their clients money.

Attorney's fees often pay for itself if the attorney will be representing you in a case with a significant amount of money on the line.

Preventative maintenance can definitely save money. Preventative maintenance for a car, air conditioner, or other mechanical device can add years onto its life. The way to determine the value of preventative maintenance for an appliance is by the following formula:

$$Cost \times Years\ Added\ /\ Lifespan$$

For example, let's say five years can be added to the life of an air conditioner with an expected lifespan of ten years, and a new air conditioner costs $4000 . The value of the preventative maintenance is $4000 x 5 / 10 = $2000. If the preventative maintenance cost is less, definitely pay for the maintenance so you can avoid purchasing a new air conditioner so soon.

Spend the money when the services allow you to earn more.

"You've got to spend money to make money." I am immediately turned off by that quote. Often the people who say that are salespeople responding to my claim that their product is too expensive. They say it in a "tsk, tsk..." tone which is very annoying.

Anyway, what is true is that <u>sometimes</u> money that you spend helps you make more money. Here, the equation is simple: Is your earnings gain from the services larger than the cost? If so, go for it.

In business, the most obvious case where this benefit can apply is in marketing, advertising, and sales.

In personal life this benefit may apply with financial coaches, therapists, education, and health care (if it can reduce your time out of work).

Spend the money when the services a professional provides is so much better than what you can do.

Let's face it. Nobody is great at everything. Some things you are great at and some things you suck at. I am great at personal finance and managing the family budget and investment portfolio. I can stretch a dollar further than anyone. I know how to get great returns on my investments at low risk. I know how to save as much as possible on taxes. I feel like I am the best in the world at this and would never outsource these duties to anyone.

Handyman work and fixing things... not so much. I suck at it. I haven't tried to fix anything for several years. The last time I did, it cost me way more in supplies and personal time than paying for the cost of a professional. And here's the thing. The professional does a way better job. Also, I tried to cut my son's hair once. Fortunately he was only five. I pay a barber for his haircuts now. Stick with your strengths. Outsource your weaknesses. You'll be much happier.

Spend the money when it provides an insurance policy.

Sometimes you don't want to take responsibility for things that go wrong. You want someone else to take responsibility. The value of eliminating the stress of responsibility can be worth a great deal. This value can make it worthwhile to pay for services you might otherwise do yourself.

This value is kind of like an insurance policy-- Usually it is a wasted expense except for the peace of mind. Occasionally it is a lifesaver and you don't know what you would have done without it.

Hiring an attorney to review a contract, paying an agent to negotiate on your behalf, maintenance inspections, and any sort of checkup (doctor, dentist, financial) fall into this category. The equation here is that the value of your peace of mind by outsourcing must be more than the cost of the service. Let someone else take on the stress.

This chapter tackles six broad categories of situations where you will choose to pay for services you do not have to. They are presented above as unique, non-overlapping situations. However in the real world many spending decisions create value in several ways. When considering paying for services, you should add the value from all the categories together. For example attorney's fees can allow you to save money on a defense case and provide an "insurance policy" in case the case goes bad.

Paying for a bookkeeper for your business can free up a big block of time to generate more sales and provide an insurance policy if things go wrong.

Anyway it's important to recognize that not all expenses are to be avoided. Some of them actually enhance your financial life.

Chapter 19 - Teaching Kids to Manage Money

Warren Buffet once said that he wants to give his kids enough of an inheritance to be able to do anything, and not so much that they can do nothing. Yes, he was talking about his billions of dollars and his adult kids. However, I believe this advice applies to families of all wealth levels and kids of all ages.

Kids should be given access to money and be given the opportunity to make money decisions as soon as they are old enough to know what money is and be able to add numbers up to ten. The first money decisions a kid can make are decisions regarding an immediate purchase-- Here's $2 you can have for treats at 7-11, you decide what to buy.

The first time I recall giving my son an opportunity to manage money was when he was either four or five and we were at the circus. I told him we could spend $10 on souvenirs and he could choose what to get. I handed him a $10 bill and watched him go to the souvenir stand. He chose a big plastic vuvuzela type horn which coincidentally cost him $10. Good for him, he made his first money decision. We went to Target the next weekend and he saw a similar plastic horn there for only $2. That purchase also taught him that "There's a sucker born every minute." That $10 paid for a very valuable lesson for him and was worth every penny for me.

The key in teaching your kids effective money management is to let your kids make stupid wasteful decisions with the money they have access to, and let them suffer the consequences of those stupid wasteful decisions. Don't overrule them, and don't bail them out. View the money you gave them and they subsequently wasted as the price you are paying to educate them about money. I'd rather have my son making stupid $2, $5, $10, and $20 money decisions now than stupid $1,000, $5,000, $10,000, and $20,000 money decisions later.

Around the same time you introduce immediate purchase decisions, you can begin to incorporate the "spend it now or later" decision. This decision is the same type of budgeting decision as the above except it is with time instead of money. Except you know from reading the prior chapters that time is money.

This decision is where you know what you are going to get, you just have to decide when you are going to get it. Sometimes there's no money even involved in a decision like that. An example is saying "You can have two candies today. You decide when you are going to eat them." Make sure you don't give extra candies if he eats them all at the beginning of the day.

Chores and privileges are a somewhat related decisions. "You have thirty minutes of chores to do. The rest of the day you can play. You decide when you are going to do your chores." Or, "You have sixty minutes of TV time, you decide how to use it." To offer this type of deal you have to be willing to step in late in the day at an inopportune time and say "you have to do your chores right now because you won't be able to finish your chores if you wait any longer". Here time is the currency that needs to be budgeted.

The next step down the road of teaching your kids how to manage money is to introduce the concept of saving. In order for a child to be able to save money, he needs to have money in the first place. Little kids don't know how to earn money, so you have to step in and make it happen. That's right, allowance.

Allowance
From my reading of literature on family finances, allowance has got to be the most controversial. There is a significant portion of personal finance experts who completely reject the whole concept of allowance. "Kids need to learn to work for their money. Giving a kid an allowance for doing nothing will kill her work ethic." they say. My response to that line of reasoning is "agree" to the first part; and "disagree" to the 2nd part. Kids have no work ethic to kill. Most kids don't have the knowledge or ability to do any productive work until they are ten or so. Besides, work ethic is developed through assigned chores. If it makes supporters of the work ethic argument feel better, they can change the word "chores" to "job duties" and change the word "allowance" to "salary".y In this book, though, I am going to use the word "allowance".

Allowance is necessary because it is a vehicle to give a child access to money and it forces a child to learn budgeting in real time. You can consider the allowance as tuition to the school of financial life. It will be the smartest tuition dollar you will ever spend.

Hopefully the last two paragraphs have solidified your conviction that allowance is an important part of parenting. The next decision to make is deciding how much allowance to give. The first basic criteria for allowance is that it has to be small enough that you can afford to pay the allowance consistently, no matter what financial disasters are occurring in your own life. If a child can't count on receiving her allowance, then it is impossible to budget and the primary value of allowance is nullified.

The next step is to decide "how much". The "how much" question is directly tied to the size of your child's financial responsibilities. You want the allowance to be large enough to cover all of your child's day to day spending and a little more to give your child the opportunity to save money or budget for bigger ticket items (e.g. a new bicycle) if things go well. Not too much more, because you want to give your child the opportunity to run out of money and experience the consequences of bad money decisions. The most important money lesson for anyone to learn is that money is finite, and it is important to save for a rainy day.

The third step is to decide how frequently you are going to give out the money-- daily, weekly, monthly... Whatever the schedule, you must communicate it to your child and live up to your side of the commitment. The older the child is, the less frequently their allowance should be handed out. Responsible children can easily handle a quarterly allowance.

The last step should be the easiest step of all. Back off! The allowance you hand your child must be unconditional. You might give suggestions based on your wisdom. However, ultimately the responsibility lies with them. Also, the suffering resulting from losing money, making poor money decisions, or just plain overspending must lie completely on their shoulders. Don't bail them out. Don't buy them treats to make up for the plan. Just help them think through how they got in the money situation they got it so they can learn the proper lessons from their mistakes. If your family sticks with this approach, you'll find your child becoming much more financially responsible

To amp up your child's financial education you can give them the opportunity to borrow and invest. Every month I give my son the opportunity to purchase a one month bond from me. The interest rate is very generous-- 10% per month. So if he pays $10 on the first of the month, he can get back $11 at the end of the month. This option requires him to really spend some time thinking about his expenses and helps him appreciate the benefits of investing. Yes, 10% a month is an extravagantly high interest rate not representative of the real world. However, I have found that real world interest rates are much too low to effectively teach a short attention span child the value of delayed gratification or investing. Even at this very high interest rate, my son seldom takes me up on my offer to sell him a bond.

He also has the opportunity to borrow from me. The cost is 20% per month. I want him to learn really early that paying interest is really punishing and something generally to be avoided.

Additional Money Rules for Kids
There shouldn't be any. Period. If your child is following external rules regarding money management, then she is not learning how to manage money, she is learning how to follow your rules. As a reminder, again, the allowance you pay your child must be unconditional. Allow your child to develop their own values and systems regarding money management. If you don't do that, then you aren't really allowing your child to learn anything about money.
So, for example, some recommend declaring a percentage of allowance must be "saved", and another percentage must be allocated to "charity". Requirements like these effectively reduce the child's allowance because they have no choice regarding what to do with that money. Go ahead and share your values. Share what you would do with the money. But don't make it a requirement to follow your

advice. Your kids need to make money decisions on their own.

Chapter 20 - Buy vs. Rent

This is a question you will face often in life. And often one of those options will be far superior in a financial sense compared to the other. Before I take you to the details of this decision process, I'll just comment on a few rules of thumb people use to help make this decision:

"Buy appreciating assets, rent depreciating assets." The idea here is that you want to own things that increase in value so you can benefit from the increase when you eventually sell them. You want to rent things that depreciate in value so you can avoid purchasing something that will eventually be worthless. This is generally a good starting point. However there are costs of ownership and benefits of renting that should also be considered.

"Buy things that you will use often; rent things you will use once in a while". Pretty self explanatory. Another good start. That's why you buy your ski jacket, but rent your ski boots. The problem with this maxim is that it is too vague to successfully apply. What does "often" or "once in a while" mean, anyway?

The two rules of thumb above are a great start. However, to do a full comparison you need to consider all of the costs and benefits, both intangible and tangible. The comparisons must consider these costs and benefits from the time of purchase to disposal. Disposal may occur when you eventually sell the product or when it ends up in the garbage.

Costs and Benefits of Buying:
If you choose to purchase, you immediately have two costs right off the bat: The hassle of buying, and the cost of buying. The hassle of buying is somewhat subjective. To me, the hassle is huge. I hate spending hours upon hours finding the best deal and then negotiating it further with the salesman of the product. As a matter of fact, the last time our family needed a car, my wife and I agreed upon a price and a week or so later she came home with a new car. My wife likes the shopping / test driving / negotiating experience. She doesn't assign much cost to the hassle of buying things. When determining the cost of buying, add in all costs related to the purchase including financing charges, sales or transfer tax, and any other required purchases at the time of purchase.

Once you get home with your new purchase, you are not done spending money on it. you have to maintain your purchase, too. If you purchase a boat, maintenance costs are kind of a big deal; if you purchase ski boots, not so much. The challenge here is that you have to forecast maintenance costs all the way out to the day you dispose of it. If a tune up for your car costs $250 and you'll need a tune up every year until it wears out in ten years, budget a $2500 cost for tune ups. Also, consider that maintenance costs increase as your purchase gets older and starts to deteriorate.

A subjective, sometimes hidden cost you have with ownership is the storage cost. The cost of storage can be objective if you are paying for a facility to store your stuff. Or it can be subjective if it is sitting around in your house taking up space that you could be using for living (or storing something else). It is possible that your storage cost is zero. This would occur if you live in a property that is so large that you have more than enough space to live and you wouldn't even notice if you lost a few more square feet to storage. Or maybe if the size of your purchase takes up so little space that its cost is insignificant. However, even if you were in that situation, there is a hidden cost for storage. In that situation, you could move to a smaller property and save on living expenses.

Most people's homes, no matter how big they are, are completely full, or overfilled (ever see the show "Hoarders"?). For those people I recommend trying to value the space that the item will be taking up. For example, owning a full set of ski equipment might take up a third of a closet in your house. How much is a closet in your house worth to you? How much would I have to pay you to rent out that closet to store my stuff? Divide the value of the closet by three and that's the storage cost for your ski equipment. Space has a premium cost in cities, so people in cities should be less interested in buying things because there is no place to put them.

The next item to consider in your purchase decision is actually a benefit. Sometimes there are added benefits to owning something as compared to renting it. Owning an item may create a sense of satisfaction, or it may have value to you because you can customize something you own to your exact specifications, or you may value having that item "on call" to be able to be used at any time, no questions asked. If any of these things have value to you, try to put a price tag on it. How much extra would you pay for a rented item that has those characteristics?

As we get to the end of the life of your purchase, there is one more cost: The hassle of selling (or getting rid of it). Often, but not always, that cost is about zero. If you are thinking "when I am tired of this purchase, I'll just throw it in the garbage," then there is no cost (and there's no resale benefit). You can do that for a set of golf clubs. You can't do that for a car.

Finally, if you expect to be able to sell your item, figure out how much you can reasonably get when your purchase is old and you don't want it anymore. Let me give you some reality check pointers. Pretty much nobody wants your old sofa that you spilled Chinese food on last year. As a matter of fact not too many people want your brand new sofa. And if they do, they won't pay more than pennies on the dollar for it; and they'll ask you to deliver it for them. If you don't believe me, check Craigslist items for sale. Now check how long the Craigslist ads have been running. Most of the time people are unable to sell their old junk. They can't sell their old junk because all the potential buyers have their own old junk that they want to get rid of. Pretty much everything you own, except for your home, vehicles, and maybe some electronics are worthless the day you are done with them. I either give away, throw out, or donate the things I am done with.

Costs and Benefits of Renting:
The costs of renting is much more straightforward. There are two - the hassle factor of going through the process of renting -- that's a time suck. Second, the actual payment for renting.

You need to compute how much money you will spend on renting over the long term. In my family we only have one car. It's gone during the day because my wife uses it for her commute. I work from home and I can get by without a car on most days. However sometimes I need a car for a business meeting or to pick my son up from school. I've been keeping track of the number of days per month I rent cars locally. It averages out to about three. The cost of three rentals is considerably cheaper than the monthly cost of car ownership.

The additional cost of renting is the hassle of actually moving your butt to the rental place and waiting in line to get and return your rental. To figure out this cost you need to compute the time it takes to go to the rental location, rent, and return the item. Then multiply that time by the value you place on your free time per hour and add that to the rental price.

There are many benefits to renting, but they are really just the flip side of the costs of ownership which was described in the last section.

Finally, the moment of truth comes. Compare the cost of ownership you computed to the cost of renting you computed. The results may surprise you but trust your numbers. Over time you'll see an improvement in your finances and your life if you go with the numbers rather than your gut.

Chapter 21- Conclusion

This book, An Adult Relationship with Money is the third in my five part series on personal finance. The topics in this book are where most personal finance books start. To me, starting with this book is kind of like starting to build a house on the third floor, or teaching algebra before multiplication. There's no way you can be successful in managing your taxes, investments, loans, and financial coaches until you have the foundation contained in the first two books. This is the book most similar to traditional personal finance books. You'll understand this book more though, because the topics in the first two books give you the foundation of financial knowledge necessary to understand personal finance. The knowledge you gather in this book will likely guide you to financial decisions in the near future that improve your finances by a few thousand dollars over the poor financial decisions you might have made without this book. Continue your journey through all five books and you'll be certain to **Never Make an Uninformed Financial Decision Again**.

Book one is titled Understanding Money. The goal of this book is to begin to get you thinking about your attitudes and beliefs regarding the basics of personal finance: Money, earning, spending, saving, and investing. In thinking about these topics, you will begin to understand how your beliefs shape your financial behaviors for better or worse. This book is the foundation for all the information and discussion contained in the remaining four books on personal finance topics that you are almost sure to face in your life.

Book two, Starting to Make Money is the second in my five part series on personal finance. The goal of this book is to get you thinking about everyday money issues that everyone faces. You learn about car loans, everyday spending and saving decisions and money issues affecting your social life. This book takes the personal finance foundation developed in Book one and applies it to the real world. After reading this book you are comfortable effectively managing your personal budget. You are generating positive cash flow in your life and are starting down a path that will lead to traditional investing and wealth building.

The fourth book is titled Now You Have Money. This book discusses financial issues and decisions you'll face if you follow the guidance in the first three books. It discusses retirement investing, annuities, and other issues related to managing a six or seven figure net worth. If you're not in that wealth category yet, you will be soon enough. Just follow the guidance from the first three books. It's great to be ahead of the game and have the peace of mind knowing how to handle your future wealth before you actually have it.

The fifth and final book is titled Extra Credit - Money for Fun. This book is the final step of the personal finance journey. Among other things, it discusses the personal finance issues around being set for life and keeping yourself educated about personal finance. If you're not set for life yet, don't fret. Just follow the guidance in the first four books and be patient. You'll make it. Think of this book as the "continuing ed" book on personal finance.

I welcome all feedback. Feel free to contact me at Hayden@ForwardFinancialPlanners.com. This is your gateway to share one-off commentary, suggestions for future books, or to get on the distribution list for updates related to future publications.

You can also subscribe to www.TypeZFinance.com for my weekly thoughts on personal finance issues that have caught my attention.

www.ingramcontent.com/pod-product-compliance
Lightning Source LLC
Chambersburg PA
CBHW072036190526
45165CB00017B/952